Contents

Look out for us. We will show you the size of every bird in this book.

Laughing cry

On the edge of a wood a sound like laughter rings out. It's a bright green woodpecker and it is searching for food.

Swoosh!

Did you know...

... A woodpecker builds its nest in a tree. It digs out a nest hole using its strong beak.

Birds

LONDON, NEW YORK, MUNICH,
MELBOURNE, and DELHI

Text by Sue Malyan
Editor Penny Smith
Senior designer Janet Allis
Publishing manager Susan Leonard
Managing art editor Clare Shedden
Jacket design Simon Oon
Picture researcher Sarah Mills
Production Luca Bazzoli
DTP Designer Almudena Díaz

First published in Great Britain in 2005 by
Dorling Kindersley Limited
80 Strand, London WC2R 0RL

A Penguin Company

2 4 6 8 10 9 7 5 3 1

Copyright © 2005 Dorling Kindersley Limited, London

A CIP catalogue record for this book
is available from the British Library.

ISBN 1-4053-1166-5

Colour reproduction by Colourscan, Singapore
Printed and bound in China by Hung Hing

Discover more at
www.dk.com

I fly to a tree then hop up the trunk holding on with my claws.

I'm feeling a bit peckish.

I use my long, sticky tongue to catch insects. Sometimes I poke my tongue into ants' nests.

These red feathers show that I'm a male. Females have black feathers here.

Green woodpeckers are 31 cm (12 in) long and can live up to 15 years.

Night watcher

At night a barn owl
watches and listens.
It is waiting for a mouse,
vole, or frog to kill and eat.

Barn owls grow to
39 cm (15 in)
long. They can live
up to 21 years.

These white feathers
help to direct sounds
into my ears.

I snatch my prey
in my sharp,
hooked talons.

I'm watching you!

Did you know...

... An owl eats its prey whole. Later it coughs up the bones, feathers, or fur in a hard lump called a pellet.

Screeeech!

My body is tiny, but my fluffy feathers make me look big.

Shy bird

At the edge of a swamp, a purple gallinule is hiding. It will dive underwater if it is frightened.

A purple gallinule can be 20 cm (8 in) long.

My feathers are coated with oil so water flows off them easily.

When I spread out my toes, I can walk on floating leaves.

I find my food in the wet ground. I eat seeds, insects, and dead fish.

I have long legs so I can wade through water.

Did you know...

... A gallinule keeps in contact with its family by making quiet clicking noises.

Just hatched

A few hours after hatching, this fluffy partridge chick is up and running about. Its stripy colouring helps it to hide in the undergrowth.

My soft, fluffy feathers are called down. They keep me lovely and warm.

A red-legged partridge chick stands at 8 cm (3 in) high. An adult grows to 34 cm (14 in).

I'll soon be growing my proper feathers, and I'll be able to fly when I'm just 16 days old.

Where's our mum got to?

I use my long toes to scratch around in the soil, looking for food.

Did you know...

... A partridge nests in a hollow in the ground. Here she lays up to 25 eggs. That's more than any other bird.

On the beach

At the seashore
oystercatchers sit in
shallow holes called
scrapes. They are
guarding their eggs.

Oystercatchers
can grow
to 45 cm
(18 in) long.

Can you spot my
eggs? They look
just like pebbles.

Did you know...

... This bird uses its beak to open shells. It prises or smashes them open and eats the soft flesh inside.

I'll be sitting here for weeks.

I don't just eat oysters – I like crabs, shrimps, and worms too!

Bird call

Screech! An eastern rosella spots danger and screeches to warn its friends. Later, it finds fruit and seeds. It calls other rosellas, inviting them to the feast.

flap! flap!

I'm a friendly bird and I live with my family. Other rosellas live with their mates.

Did you know...

... A rosella's beak never stops growing. It is worn into shape cracking nuts and seeds.

I'm a male. My brightly coloured feathers help me attract a female.

crack crack crunch!

The eastern rosella can grow to 60 cm (2 ft) long.

First feathers

High up in an oak tree, a young tawny owl sits quietly. Its mottled feathers blend in with the branches and leaves, making it difficult to be seen.

Tawny owls grow up to 39 cm (15 in).

I have soft downy feathers because I am a young bird.

Did you know...

... An owl can look behind it by turning its head right round so it faces backwards.

My feathers have fluffy edges that help me to fly silently.

hoo-hooo

Feathers on my toes protect me from the bites of my prey.

Enormous bill

In the hot, wet rainforest, a Cuvier's toucan is having a snack. It uses its bill to break into a sweet passionfruit. Yum! Yum!

slurp slurp

My bill is nearly as big as my body, but it's very light because it's hollow.

A toucan's bill can be 12 cm (5 in) long.

When I eat, I lift up my bill and tip food down my throat.

21

Did you know...

... When a toucan wants to sleep, it rests its bill on its back, then nods off.

Passionfruit's my favourite!

You recognize your friends by their faces, but I know mine by their colourful bills.

Grab a snack

From the edge of a stream, a grey wagtail darts out. It grabs a fly in its beak and holds on to the wriggling insect.

My tail helps
me steer
when I fly.

Did you know...

... When a wagtail perches, it tail bobs up and down. This is why it is called a wagtail.

I carry dirt from my nest and drop it in the stream.